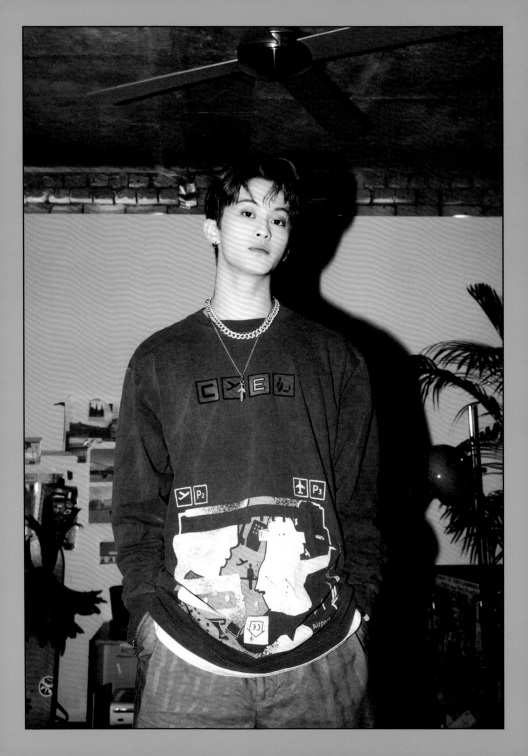

RENJUN
JENO

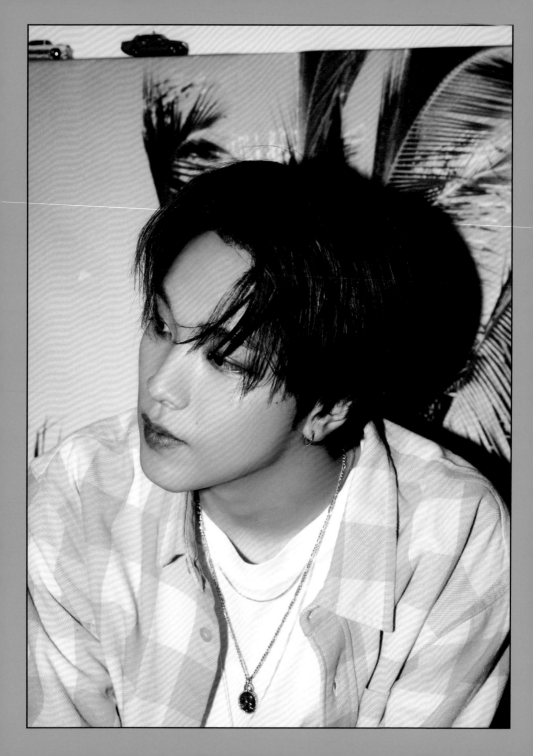

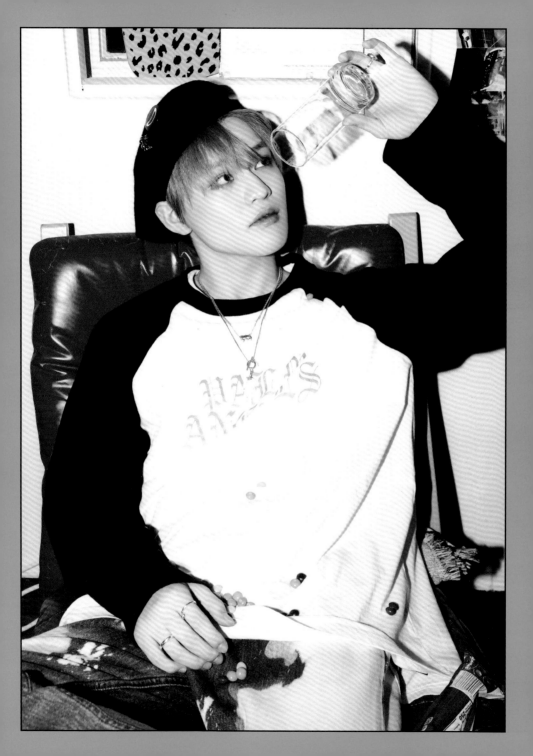

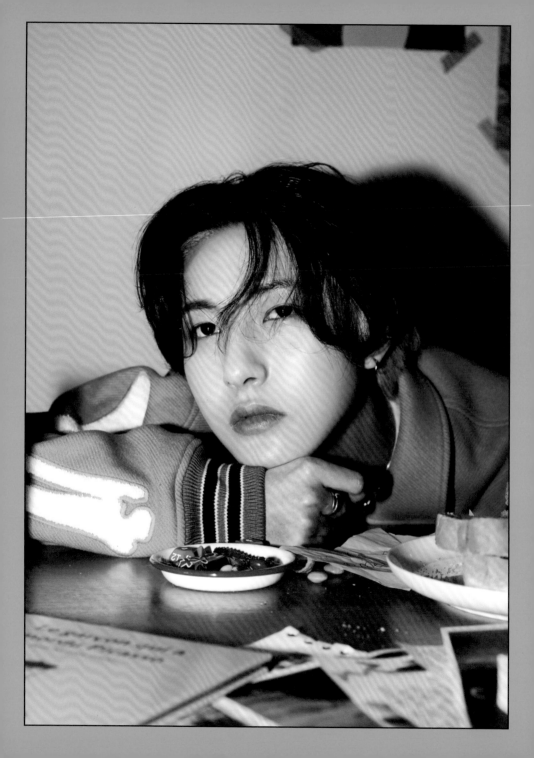

맛
(Hot Sauce)

Hot sauce 깊이 dip that eh 날 따라 넌 twist that eh Hot sauce 타오를 때 ooh 입맛대로 골라 ma dish

넌 뭐가 궁금해 나는 너만의 chef 이건 너를 위한 plate yeah
내가 맛 보여 줄게 시간은 충분해 지금 우리 눈치도 보지 마
그저 taste it 내 비법은 색다른 spicy 살짝만 스쳐도 정신없지
설탕이 발린 맛엔 이내 질리기 쉬워 뜨거운 나의 feelin'
지금 느꼈지 넌 너와 내 사이 선명히 보인 커져만 가는 열기
난 오감을 깨워 네 맘을 깨워 터질 것만 같은 ma skill

골라 ma dish 골라 ma dish 골라 ma dish Hot sauce
깊이 dip that eh 날 따라 넌 twist that eh Hot sauce
타오를 때 ooh 입맛대로 골라 ma dish

아예 방심 하지마 uh 빈틈이 없을 테니까 Yeah 넌 자극적인
내 감각 ooh 가능하겠니 감당 nope Yeah yeah 버틸 턱이
없잖아 nah 긴장을 더 풀고서 넌 bon appétit now that's
right 주체 못 해 자꾸 빠져드는 맛 cuz you can't stop
난 끝까지 get ya 찾게 될 걸 every day (and every
night) 중독돼 이미 넌 네 맘을 더 섞어봐 (이젠 남김없이)
계속 원하게 돼 어지런 머리 네 두 손발이 이끌려 내게 이미
좀 더 자극적일 매 순간들이 강렬해 what we gon' eat

골라 ma dish (I'm the one what you want what you
want what you want ah ya) 골라 ma dish (I'm the
one what you want what you want what you want
ah ya) 골라 ma dish Hot sauce 깊이 dip that eh
날 따라 넌 twist that eh Hot sauce 타오를 때 ooh
입맛대로 골라 ma dish

너를 삼켜버린 feelin' 사로잡은 이런 끌림 뗄 수가 없잖아
좀 더 깊이 빠져들 때 원해 원해 원해봐 더 babe 얼마든지
더 바래 바래 babe 너의 혀끝 위로 아른거릴 완벽해진 맛을
즐겨 You want it babe

(I'm the one what you want what you want what
you want ah ya) 골라 ma dish (I'm the one what
you want what you want what you want ah ya)
골라 ma dish Hot sauce 깊이 dip that eh 날 따라 넌
twist that eh Hot sauce 타오를 때 ooh 입맛대로 골라
ma dish

TRACK   No.1

Korean Lyrics by
문여름 (JamFactory) / 조윤경

Composed by
Martin Wave / Tinashe Sibanda / Philip Kembo /
Rosina "Soaky Siren" Russell / John Mitchell /
Ninos Hanna / YOO YOUNG JIN

Arranged by
Martin Wave / Bantu / Dr. Chaii / YOO YOUNG JIN

Vocal Directed by
KENZIE / YOO YOUNG JIN

Background Vocals by
NCT 해찬 / NCT 런쥔 / JUNNY

Recorded by
노민지 @ SM Yellow Tail Studio /
YOO YOUNG JIN @ SM BOOMINGSYSTEM

Digital Editing by
정유라 /
YOO YOUNG JIN @ SM BOOMINGSYSTEM

Engineered for Mix by
노민지 @ SM Yellow Tail Studio /
YOO YOUNG JIN @ SM BOOMINGSYSTEM

Mixed by
정의석 @ SM Blue Cup Studio

Original Title
Calamari

Original Writers
Martin Wave / Johnny Yukon (John Mitchelle) /
Soaky Siren (Rosina Russell) / T-Collar (Tinashe
Sibanda) / Pip Kembo (Philip Kembo)

Original Publishers
SILO Music / Ultra Empire Music (BMI) / Ultra Music
Publishing Europe AG (SUISA) / Artist 101 Publishing
Group / Prescription Songs LLC / Where Da Kasz At /
Artist 101 Publishing Group administered by Kobalt
Music Publishing Ltd (KMP)

Sub-Publisher
Music Cube, Inc.

Ah ha boom Diggity I got some serious Diggity 틀림없는
신호 귓속에 쿵쿵댄 심포니 I know it's time for Diggity

혼자이던 시간이 밤이 이제 곧 끝나 붉어지는 태양이 내게
말을 걸어와 얼마나 긴 시간 흘렀어 하품하며 기지개를 켜
'Cause we gon' make it hot hot 돛을 높이 올리자 Huh
huh take it down 서랍 속 넣어 둔 기억들이 책갈피 사이
끼워 둔 꿈이 내게 다가왔어 'Fly to the sky!' Diggity

*Come in hard boom Diggity 난 멈추지 않아 We go
far boom Diggity wow wow wow boom diggy
diggy 우리 시간들은 별들을 지나치며 아주 천천히 가지 세찬
바람맞으면 살아있다는 걸 느끼지 Come in hard boom
Diggity Diggity

Hey 너와 바다를 건너는 상상해 우린 위험한 여행을 떠나
그래 마주 보고 oh 좀 더 무모한 걸음을 걷고 Turn up the
volume now 부싯돌처럼 불꽃을 피워 거침없이 가는 난
콜럼버스 세상의 끝을 넘어 더 멀리 가고 싶어 금빛의 수평선
눈부셔 나를 지켜봐 봐 바람이 바뀌는 걸 느끼자 소리치는
고동을 들어봐 이제 시간이야 'Fly to the sky!' Diggity
Klickidyklock tippity tap all of my life yeah 기억해 줘
언제나 함께 이길 원한 날 둘이서 바라본 꿈들 언제나 멋지잖아
누군가 미쳤다 해도 We get Diggity

*Repeat

내 삶을 위해 난 싸울 거야 난 이 삶과의 사랑에 빠진 거니까
세상이 내 품에 있어 과거도 미래도 즐기고 있을 거야 Look
at me 날 따라와 봐 look at me Diggity

*Repeat

Diggity

TRACK	No.2

Korean Lyrics by

KENZIE

Composed by

KENZIE / Moonshine / Cazzi Opeia

Arranged by

Moonshine

Vocal Directed by

KENZIE

Background Vocals by

NCT DREAM / Cazzi Opeia

Recorded by

이지홍 @ SM LVYIN Studio /

권유진 @ doobdoob Studio

Digital Editing by

이지홍 @ SM LVYIN Studio

Engineered for Mix by

이민규 @ SM Big Shot Studio

Mixed by

정의석 @ SM Blue Cup Studio

Original Title

DIGGITY

Original Writers

KENZIE / Jonatan Gusmark / Ludvig Evers /

Moa Anna Carlebecker Forsell

Original Publishers

EKKO Music Rights (powered by CTGA) /

EKKO Music Rights Europe (powered by CTGA)

Sub-Publisher

EKKO Music Rights (powered by CTGA)

고래
(Dive Into You)

TRACK   No.3

Korean Lyrics by

Ellie Suh (153 Joombas)

Composed by

David Wilson / Wyatt Sanders / James Abrahart

Arranged by

dwilly

Vocal Directed by

주찬양 (ICONIC SOUNDS)

Background Vocals by

주찬양 (ICONIC SOUNDS) / James Abrahart /
Wyatt Sanders

Recorded by

권유진 @ doobdoob Studio / 강은미 @ SM
SSAM Studio / 정호진 @ sound POOL studios

Digital Editing by

노민지 @ SM Yellow Tail Studio

Engineered for Mix by

이지홍 @ SM LVYIN Studio

Mixed by

김철순 @ SM Blue Ocean Studio

Original Title

DIE4YOU 2

Original Writers

David Wilson / Wyatt Sanders /
James Abrahart

Original Publishers

Pelvic Thrust Music / These Are Songs of Pulse /
Concord Sound / Wop De Gang /
Artist Publishing Group West (ASCAP) /
Let's Get Brunch Publishing /
Artist 101 Publishing Group (BMI) administered
by Kobalt Music Publishing Ltd (KMP)

Sub-Publishers

Fujipacific Music Korea Inc. / Music Cube, Inc.

Look around 둘러봐도 온통 짙은 푸른빛 까만 밤 마치 깊은 물에 잠수한 듯이 먹먹함 속에 너의 목소리만 뚜렷해 어쩌지 나에게 넌 달아나는 저 수평선 같지 눈앞에 너를 두고서도 나는 또다시 그리워 너는 파도처럼 나를 삼키지 어쩌지 Oh you and I 넌 아득한 나의 바다 난 너의 품에 빠져 You and I 너에게 가 닿고 싶어

*I will dive into you you I will dive into you you I will dive into you

궁금해 네 맘 한가운데 나는 어딘지 표류해 모르는 채 한번 가보는 거지 막막해 가끔 이 마음의 끝은 어딜지 너인지 심각해 널 스치는 바람마저 질투해 네 뺨에 내려앉는 달빛도 annoying me 그보다 더 가까이 내가 곁에 있을래 가까이 Oh you and I 넌 유일한 나의 바다 난 너의 눈에 잠겨 You and I 그 안에 난 살고 싶어

*Repeat **Swim down 두 눈앞이 파랗게 Swim down 네 안에서 난 꿈을 꿔 you I will dive into you

Sail 떠도는 바다 위의 whale 늘 바랬어 머물기를 매일 외로운 낮과 긴 밤을 나 찾아 헤맸던 건 너였음을 이제는 나 알 것 같애 네가 날 숨 쉬게 한단 걸 yea yea 너에게 너의 안에 너를 향해 가는 항해 I will dive I will dive I will dive into you

*Repeat **Repeat

You and I 나의 바다 포근한 품 I will dive into you

눈을 감아봐 선명하게 번져 My youth 나를 데려가 기억
한켠 너에게로 그 눈부신 한때 그날의 우리 뜨거웠던 날
밤하늘에 수놓은 꿈 너와 나의 빛나는 youth

넌 지금 뭐 해 어떻게 지내? 가끔은 너도 내 생각해?
한여름 태양 같았던 우리 그 반짝임에 잠시 기대 다친
마음도 낫게 해 생각만으로 또 두근대 기억나 you and
me 서투르고 찬란했지 아름다웠어 우리 나눴던 순간들
밤하늘 가득 밝게 비춰

*그때 너와 나 별빛 위에 그렸던 꿈 아름다워 다 함께 울고
웃던 기억 그 눈부신 한때 그날의 우리 뜨거웠던 날 잊지
못할 거야 전부 기억해 줘 우리의 youth

처음 느끼는 감정에 빠져 다른 건 보이지 않았지 그 마음만큼
쓰렸던 so long 아팠던 만큼 추억이 돼 지나간 시간 속에
돌아갈 수 없기에 그렇기에 (그래) 더욱더 소중한가 봐 너는
나의 봄이고 여름 축제는 끝났어도 내게 남아있어 그날에
봤던 불꽃처럼

*Repeat

우리 이다음 만났을 때 웃으면서 인사하기로 해 나의
전부였던 너 늘 함께한 우리 둘 그 기억 하나면 돼 난 이 돌고
도는 계절 속에 물든 너를 기억해 우릴 기억해 오래도록

눈을 감아봐 선명하게 번져 My youth 아름다워 다 함께
울고 웃던 기억 그 눈부신 한때 그날의 우리 마음속에 다
깊이 간직하게 모두 너와 나의 빛나는 youth

우리의 계절
(My Youth)

TRACK	No. 4
Korean Lyrics by	
이지윤 (JamFactory)	
Composed by	
David Wilson / Wyatt Sanders / Scott Effman	
Arranged by	
dwilly	
Vocal Directed by	
Kriz	
Background Vocals by	
NCT 천러 / NCT 런쥔 / NCT 마크 / NCT 해찬	
Recorded by	
권유진 @ doobdoob Studio	
Digital Editing by	
권유진 @ doobdoob Studio	
Engineered for Mix by	
강은지 @ SM SSAM Studio	
Mixed by	
남궁진 @ SM Concert Hall Studio	
Original Title	
RECKLESS	
Original Writers	
David Wilson / Wyatt Sanders / Scott Effman	
Original Publishers	
Pelvic Thrust Music / These are Songs of Pulse /	
Concord Sounds / Artist Publishing Group	
West administered by Kobalt Music Publishing	
Ltd (KMP) / Skyfolk Songs /	
Concord Sounds admin by Peermusic (Various)	
Sub-Publishers	
Fujipacific Music Korea Inc. / Music Cube, Inc.	

Rocket

차가웠던 내 발밑에 불이 붙어올 때까지 헬륨을 압축하듯
우린 터질 것 같아 It's real yeah Yeah 달아올라
폭발하기 직전 거세진 맘의 떨림마다 눈부신 불꽃들이 튀어
힘껏 날아올라 볼까 babe 온 우주가 우릴 위한 무대야
더없이 충분한 energy babe

*Ooh ah 뜨겁게 타올라 Ooh ah time for shot
무거웠던 맘들을 하나씩 떨치고 난 하늘 높이 발사된
Rocket 네 목소린 countdown Rock the world like a
fireball Ooh ah 궤도를 벗어나 예측할 수 없는 Dream
Rocket

눈앞엔 온통 star wars 상상해 light saber 별빛마저
가를 거야 Level up level up level up level up 미지의
곳에서 일렁이는 fire Boom boom 터트려 난 all night
Zoom zoom 쉴 새 없는 spotlight 온 우주가 두 발아래
무대야 한계를 넘어선 gravity babe

*Repeat

닿을 수 없던 대기권을 지나 숨이 가빠 오는 순간 (펼쳐지는
빛) I'm taking you higher 멈추지 않을 너와 나 oh

**전혀 다른 차원에서 만나 babe 그 누구도 이젠 우릴
감당 못해 온 세상을 다 지금 막 터트려 대

Ooh ah 더 밝게 타올라 Ooh ah time for shot 빨라지는
속도에 모든 걸 맡기고 난 거침없이 발사된 Rocket
앞질러 봐 countdown Rock the world like a fireball
Ooh ah 궤도가 돼 볼까 매일 밤 널 이끌 Dream Rocket

**Repeat

가장 밝게 빛나는 Rocket 달아오른 이 느낌을 따라 babe
쉴 새 없이 어디로든 발사 해대 갇혀있던 맘 모두 다 터트려
대 가장 높이 빛날 Dream Rocket

TRACK   No. 5

Korean Lyrics by
조윤경

Composed by
Moonshine / Misunderstood / Realmeee

Arranged by
Moonshine

Vocal Directed by
Realmeee

Background Vocals by
JUNNY

Recorded by
권유진 @ doobdoob Studio

Digital Editing by
강은지 @ SM SSAM Studio

Engineered for Mix by
강은지 @ SM SSAM Studio

Mixed by
이민규 @ SM Big Shot Studio

Original Title
Bodyrock (Earthquake)

Original Writers
Jonatan Gusmark / Ludvig Evers / Realmeee /
Stephan Lee Benson / Jeffrey Okyere-Twusami

Original Publishers
EKKO Music Rights Europe (powered by CTGA) /
EKKO Music Rights (powered by CTGA) /
Create Future

Sub-Publisher
EKKO Music Rights (powered by CTGA)

Yeah you know what time it is This one's gonna be explosive 한 번 불 붙이면 끝을 보지 확 터져버릴 그때까지 누가 우릴 막아 show is ready Top floor딛고 sky까지 We're upgrading 불꽃이 튀는 순간 시작되는 Countdown 완벽히 잠들었던 이 공간을 깨 흔들어 느껴져 closely 더 헐거워진 안전핀 yeah yeah yeah 꽉 묶인 난 control freak 풀린 그 순간 yeah yeah yeah 꿈결 속에 아른대던 장면들이 불길처럼 눈앞에 확 번질 테니 일 초가 일 분 같던 찰나가 영원 같던 까맣게 애태운 그 시간을 지나 터질 듯 달아올라 난 지금 We the bomb 'bout to blow 불 붙여봐

*We might explode 갇혔던 꿈 타올라 더 my mind go boom Our time goes Tick ey ey 더 뜨거워 터질 듯 뜨거워 Now we're so dangerous Yeah we're so dangerous

Yeah you know you know you know 뭘 고민해 이미 멈출 수 없는 playing 파편이 되어 빗발친 Something like thrill ooh ooh ooh What's crazy? 부서진 cage 치솟는 gauge We're so crazy now 이건 마치 화염 위로 쏟아진 missile 아무리 터뜨리고 태워내도 끝없는 기분 반응한 맘을 따라 무너진 너의 fire line 걷잡을 수도 없이 번져온 순간 더 이상 물러설 곳은 없어 We the bomb 'bout to blow 불 태워봐

*Repeat

이 순간을 기억해 초침 소릴 들어 봐 뛰는 심장 속에 들이쳐 요동치는 저 시간 끝에서 우린 충돌할지 몰라 0초가 된 그 순간 Get it down get it down get it down get it down down down 빠르게 바뀌는 빨간 numbers on the board 0이 되는 순간엔 어쩔 수 없는걸 I've been waiting for this time 터져버릴 듯한 마음 이 정도면 오래도 참았어 tic toc Tic tic tic toc Everybody get down 뒤로 빠져 휩싸여 위험해 진짜로 Tic tic tic toc 4 3 2 1 끝나버린 Countdown Drop a bomb on you baby oh

We'll all explode 바로 지금 터질수록 커지는 꿈 Our time goes Tick 내 안의 날 깨워 Now we're so dangerous Yeah we're so dangerous Now we're so dangerous

Countdown
(3, 2, 1)

TRACK	No. 6

Korean Lyrics by

장정원 (JamFactory) / Rick Bridges (X&)

Composed by

Moonshine / DEEZ / Bobii Lewis / Rick Bridges (X&)

Arranged by

Moonshine

Vocal Directed by

DEEZ

Background Vocals by

주찬양 (ICONIC SOUNDS)

Recorded by

권유진 @ doobdoob Studio /

강은지 @ SM SSAM Studio /

정호진 @ sound POOL studios

Digital Editing by

권유진 @ doobdoob Studio

Engineered for Mix by

강은지 @ SM SSAM Studio

Mixed by

남궁진 @ SM Concert Hall Studio

Original Title

TICK TICK

Original Writers

Jonatan Gusmark / Ludvig Evers /

DEEZ / Bobii Lewis

Original Publishers

EKKO Music Rights Europe (powered by CTGA) /

EKKO Music Rights (powered by CTGA)

Sub-Publisher

EKKO Music Rights (powered by CTGA)

ANL

네가 어디서 무얼 하든 어딜 가든 oh 내 머릿속엔 너가 있어 I'm sorry I beg your pardon? oh 네 생각하다가 또 놓쳤어 내 모든 순간을 책임지는 scene May I take your picture? 찰칵하고 터뜨린 flash I just go with the flow we call it Love it's natural baby 내게 흘러와 별 볼일 없던 장면을 채웠어 your appearance 하늘 위에 달같이 너는 매일 밤 떠오르네

*All Night Long 아무것도 못해 난 I don't care All Night Long 두 눈을 감아도 넓은 하늘에 너를 그릴래 별들을 이어 이름을 붙였지 난 All Night Long Yeah yeah we can paint all day 그래 완벽해

Take it 밤하늘의 moonlight Take it 그 옆에의 starlight Yeah I'll give it to you every night 너와 해가 질 때까지 sky high 내 마음의 규칙을 알잖아 오직 예외인 건 너잖아 Look at my face It's not a game 손을 잡아 babe 널 놓칠 일은 없어 no way Yeah 보이는 대로 믿고 싶어서 난 눈을 감았어 잠이 오질 않아서 난 꿈을 내가 그렸 uh yeah 아무도 없는 곳에 우리 둘뿐였음해 네 생각이 아침까지 베개가 돼 my babe Where you at 내 시간을 다 가져줘 너의 마음 앞에 툭 던지고 왔어 밤은 꿈 속에 우릴 이어주는 bridge 하늘 위에 달 나를 떠올려줘

*Repeat

오늘인듯해 드디어 너와 내가 oh underneath the same light 오직 너여야만 해 even if there ain't no time Just take my hand and just fly Yeah yeah 검은 미로 속 불빛은 바로 너였어 내 다른 이름 하늘 너의 옆에 적었어 별다른 이유 없이 너에게 끌렸듯 저기 저 별의 뜻은 I'm yours and you are mine 바뀐 게 하나도 없지 네 주위를 공전해 달같이 너의 밤은 so speedy girl Mr. time just wait for me please I wanna be your sunrise girl

All Night Long 밤새도록 생각해 I don't care All Night Long 두 눈을 감아도 넓은 하늘에 너를 그릴래 별들을 이어 이름을 붙였지 난 All Night Long Yeah yeah we can paint all day 그래 완벽해

TRACK   No.7

Lyrics by

jane / ron / 그리즐리 / 크래커 / JUNNY / 이아일

Composed by

no2zcat / 이아일 / JUNNY / ron

Arranged by

no2zcat

Vocal Directed by

JUNNY / ron / no2zcat

Background Vocals by

JUNNY / NCT 해찬

Recorded by

권유진 @ doobdoob Studio

Digital Editing by

노민지 @ SM Yellow Tail Studio

Engineered for Mix by

강은지 @ SM SSAM Studio

Mixed by

김철순 @ SM Blue Ocean Studio

Original Title

ANL

Original Writers

no2zcat / Grizzly / CRACKER / 이아일 (oiaisle) /
JUNNY / jane / ron

Original Publishers

Copyright Control (KOMCA) / EKKO Music Rights
(powered by CTGA) / Sony Music Publishing
Korea

HOT SAUCE

주인공
(Irreplaceable)

Irreplaceable Irreplaceable 아주 오랜 얘기처럼 당연한 것들이 있어 누구든 똑같이 답할 수 있는 그런 질문 말해서 뭐해 줄리엣은? 로미오 당연히 미녀 하면? 야수고 날 보면 먼저 사람들은 떠올려 너의 이름 I wanna tell you love to you 아무도 바꿀 수 없게 그렇게 정해진 거야 love you 24/7 나의 주인공

*항상 우린 Irreplaceable 난 널 사랑이라 불러 아주 작은 순간조차 벅찬 의민 걸 내 모든 이야기는 봐도 봐도 너인 거야 내 주인공 꼭 뗄 수 없는 한 문장처럼 Irreplaceable

너와는 어디라도 헤맨대도 명장면 오히려 예고 없이 펼쳐질 많은 일들이 두근거려 Yeah 까맣게 물든 밤 조용히 잠든 도시 starring 너와 나 시작돼버린 movie 깜빡거리는 가로등마저 spotlight처럼 느껴지게 해 주변이 반짝거려 너와의 모든 순간 영화 속의 장면처럼 머릿속에 지나가고 와있어 이제 climax 대사처럼 수천 번은 연습했던 말 넌 내 삶의 주인공 널 담고 싶어 영원히 I wanna tell you love to you 누구도 채울 수 없는 네 자린 대체 불가야 너만이 나의 유일한 주인공

*Repeat

너로 인해 너의 너로부터 널 위해 이루어진 모든 감정 짧은 순간 넌 내 시가 되고 나를 눈물 나게 해 Irreplaceable babe 이리 아름다워 넌 baby 이야긴 너로서 완성돼 you're the Irreplaceable Take 1 자연스럽게 잡은 두 손 Take 2 입가에 미소 in close up Take 3 살랑이는 breeze so sweet Take 4 yeah we 'bout to hug & kiss Bravo! 어떤 각도 어떤 장면에서도 너무 완벽해서 we can win another Oscar I'll tell you love to you Irreplaceable

*Repeat

Irreplaceable babe Irreplaceable babe Irreplaceable babe Irreplaceable babe

TRACK   No. 8

Korean Lyrics by
조아영 (153 Joombas) / Rick Bridges (X&)

Composed by
DEEZ / The Family / Rick Bridges (X&)

Arranged by
DEEZ

Vocal Directed by
DEEZ

Background Vocals by
변장문 / DEEZ

Recorded by
권유진 @ doobdoob Studio

Digital Editing by
권유진 @ doobdoob Studio

Engineered for Mix by
이민규 @ SM Big Shot Studio

Mixed by
이지홍 @ SM LVYIN Studio

Original Title
Irreplaceable

Original Writers
DEEZ / Joy Deb / Linnea Deb / Anton Hård af Segerstad

Original Publishers
EKKO Music Rights (powered by CTGA) / Northbound Publishing adm. by Universal Music Publishing

Sub-Publisher
Universal Music Publishing Korea

지금 처럼만

(Be There For You)

혹시 기억해 처음 만난 햇살 가득히 눈부셨던 그날 늘 이렇게 나의 곁에 있어준 너에게 난 감사해 and again and again I just need you to be with me As time goes on 우리 편해진 게 때론 속상하게 했을지 몰라 언제든 내게 말해도 돼 네가 원하는 내가 돼줄게

*너의 하루 끝엔 늘 내가 가득 널 품에 안고 네 얘길 들어줄게 내겐 항상 완벽하지 않아도 돼 it's alright 넌 이대로 있어주면 돼 늘 지금처럼만 늘 지금처럼만

As time goes on 익숙해져 버린 우리라서 나는 더 다행인걸 언제든 내가 돌아 보면 그 자리에 있을 널 알기에

*Repeat

내가 늘 꿈꿔왔던 세상을 선물해 준 너 I always wanna be there for you and I know that you will feel the same

나의 하루 끝엔 네가 가득 날 품에 안고 내 얘길 들어줄래 우리 항상 완벽하지 않아도 돼 it's alright 넌 이대로 있어주면 돼 늘 지금처럼만 넌 내 곁에 있어주면 돼 지금처럼만

TRACK   No. 9

Lyrics by
밍지션 (minGtion) / JUNNY

Composed by
밍지션 (minGtion) / JUNNY

Arranged by
밍지션 (minGtion)

Vocal Directed by
밍지션 (minGtion)

Background Vocals by
JUNNY

Piano Performed by
밍지션 (minGtion)

Guitar Performed by
박신원

Bass Performed by
밍지션 (minGtion)

Recorded by
노민지 @ SM Yellow Tail Studio /
이민규 @ SM Big Shot Studio

Digital Editing by
밍지션 (minGtion)

Engineered for Mix by
노민지 @ SM Yellow Tail Studio

Mixed by
김철순 @ SM Blue Ocean Studio

Original Title
지금처럼만

Original Writers
minGtion / JUNNY

Original Publishers
EKKO Music Rights (powered by CTGA) /
Sony Music Publishing Korea